Tomie dePaola's BOOK OF POEMS

Methuen Children's Books

London

First published in Great Britain in 1989
by Methuen Children's Books Ltd
Michelin House
81 Fulham Road, London SW3 6RB
Illustrations copyright © 1988 by Tomie dePaola
Published by arrangement with G. P. Putnam's Sons
Book design by Nanette Stevenson.
Calligraphy by Jeanyee Wong.
ISBN 0-416-13272-3

For Arthur Levine
   who helped so much on this book

For Nora Cohen
   who helps on all of them

                    —TdeP

Contents

There Is No Frigate Like a Book *Emily Dickinson* 9

from Songs of Innocence *William Blake* 11

from The Way to Start a Day *Byrd Baylor* 12

Time to Rise *Robert Louis Stevenson* 13

Cat Kisses *Bobbi Katz* 13

Song *Nootka* 14

Celebration *Alonzo Lopez* 15

The Storm *Dorothy Aldis* 16

Windy Nights *Robert Louis Stevenson* 17

Brooms *Dorothy Aldis* 18

Rain of Leaves *Aileen Fisher* 19

Haiku *Gaki* 19

hose *Valerie Worth* 20

Bubbles *Carl Sandburg* 21

The Secret Place *Tomie dePaola* 22

Secret Door *Myra Cohn Livingston* 23

The Island *Dorothy Aldis* 24

Hideout *Aileen Fisher* 25

We're Racing, Racing down the Walk *Phyllis McGinley* 26

All Wet *Tony Johnston* 27

Overdog *Tony Johnston* 28

Queenie *Leland B. Jacobs* 29

The Witch *Jack Prelutsky* 30

Ghoulies and Ghosties *Old spell* 31

My Brother *Dorothy Aldis* 31

A Good Play *Robert Louis Stevenson* 32

back yard *Valerie Worth* 33

Worlds I Know *Myra Cohn Livingston* 34

The Walrus and the Carpenter *Lewis Carroll* 36

A House of Cards *Christina Rossetti* 42

from Teddy Bear *A. A. Milne* 42

Silly Song *Frederico Garcia Lorca* 43

Cancion Tonta *Frederico Garcia Lorca* 43

Hallowe'en Indignation Meeting *Margaret Fishback* 44

The Moon's the North Wind's Cooky *Vachel Lindsay* 46

Old Man Moon *Aileen Fisher* 47

from The Wind and the Moon *George MacDonald* 47

Bananas and Cream *David McCord* 48

The Little Girl and the Turkey *Dorothy Aldis* 49

Places to Hide a Secret Message *Eve Merriam* 49

The Land of Counterpane *Robert Louis Stevenson* 51

Brother *Mary Ann Hoberman* 52

Little *Dorothy Aldis* 53

Some Things Don't Make Any Sense at All *Judith Viorst* 53

basketball *Nikki Giovanni* 54

Mother to Son *Langston Hughes* 55

To a Forgetful Wishing Well *X. J. Kennedy* 56

Poem *Langston Hughes* 56

A Small Discovery *James A. Emanuel* 57

The Sugar Lady *Frank Asch* 58

Growing Old *Rose Henderson* 58

Dunce Song 6 *Mark Van Doren* 59

Old Noah's Ark *Folk rhyme* 61

The Song of the Mischievous Dog *Dylan Thomas* 62

The Panther *Ogden Nash* 63

I Speak, I Say, I Talk *Arnold L. Shapiro* 64

Eagle Flight *Alonzo Lopez* 65

The Blackbird *Humbert Wolfe* 65

The Song of the Jellicles *T. S. Eliot* 66

Alligator on the Escalator *Eve Merriam* 68

Ground Hog Day *Lilian Moore* 70

Singing *Dorothy Aldis* 71

Dandelion *Hilda Conkling* 71

The Three Foxes *A. A. Milne* 73

Busy Summer *Aileen Fisher* 74

Open Hydrant *Marci Ridlon* 75

The Balloon Man *Dorothy Aldis* 76

The Hungry Waves *Dorothy Aldis* 77

The Caterpillar *Christina Rossetti* 78

Haiku *Yayû* 78

Snail *Frederico Garcia Lorca* 79

Caracola *Frederico Garcia Lorca* 79

Cat in Moonlight *Douglas Gibson* 80

Fog *Carl Sandburg* 81

Flowers at Night *Aileen Fisher* 81

The Swallow *Christina Rossetti* 82

Autumn Leaves *Aileen Fisher* 82

Dragon Smoke *Lilian Moore* 83

Autumn *Emily Dickinson* 83

Stopping By Woods on a Snowy Evening *Robert Frost* 84

City Lights *Rachel Field* 86

Window *Carl Sandburg* 86

Dream Variation *Langston Hughes* 87

Bed in Summer *Robert Louis Stevenson* 88

Covers *Nikki Giovanni* 89

Little Donkey Close Your Eyes *Margaret Wise Brown* 90

Copyright Acknowledgments 92

Index of First Lines 94

There is no frigate like a book
To take us lands away
Nor any coursers like a page
Of prancing poetry–
This traverse may the poorest take
Without oppress of toll–
How frugal is the chariot
That bears the human soul.

— *Emily Dickinson*

from Songs of Innocence

Piping down the valleys wild
Piping songs of pleasant glee
On a cloud I saw a child,
And he laughing said to me,

"Pipe a song about a Lamb";
So I piped with merry cheer.
"Piper pipe that song again"—
So I piped, he wept to hear.

"Drop thy pipe thy happy pipe
Sing thy songs of happy cheer";
So I sung the same again
While he wept with joy to hear.

"Piper sit thee down and write
In a book that all may read"—
So he vanished from my sight.
And I plucked a hollow reed,

And I made a rural pen,
And I stained the water clear,
And I wrote my happy songs
Every child may joy to hear.

— *William Blake*

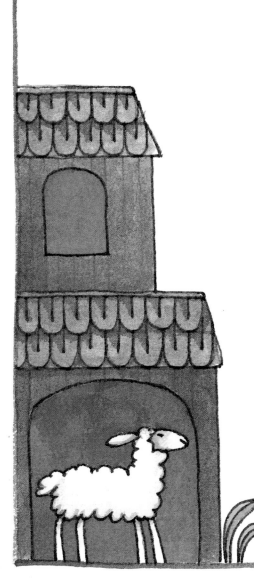

from The Way to Start a Day

The way to start a day
is this—

Go outside
and face the east
and greet the sun
with some kind of
blessing
or chant
or song
that you made yourself
and keep for
early morning.

— *Byrd Baylor*

Time to Rise

A birdie with a yellow bill
Hopped upon the window sill,
Cocked his shining eye and said:
"Ain't you 'shamed, you sleepyhead!"

— *Robert Louis Stevenson*

Cat Kisses

Sandpaper kisses
on a cheek or a chin—
that is the way
for a day to begin!

Sandpaper kisses—
a cuddle, a purr.
I have an alarm clock
that's covered with fur.

— *Bobbi Katz*

Song

Don't you ever
you up in the sky
don't you ever get tired
of having the clouds
between you and us?

— *Nootka*

Celebration

I shall dance tonight.
When the dusk comes crawling,
There will be dancing
   and feasting.
I shall dance with the others
   in circles,
     in leaps,
       in stomps.
Laughter and talk
   will weave into the night,
Among the fires
   of my people.
Games will be played
And I shall be
   a part of it.

— Alonzo Lopez

The Storm

In my bed all safe and warm
I like to listen to the storm.
The thunder rumbles loud and grand—
The rain goes splash and whisper; and
The lightning is so sharp and bright
It sticks its fingers through the night.

— *Dorothy Aldis*

Windy Nights

Whenever the moon and stars are set,
　　Whenever the wind is high,
All night long in the dark and wet,
　　A man goes riding by.
Late in the night when the fires are out,
Why does he gallop and gallop about?

Whenever the trees are crying aloud,
　　And ships are tossed at sea,
By, on the highway, low and loud
　　By at the gallop goes he.
By at the gallop goes he, and then
By he comes back at the gallop again.

　　　　　— *Robert Louis Stevenson*

Brooms

On stormy days
When the wind is high,
Tall trees are brooms
Sweeping the sky.

They swish their branches
In buckets of rain
And swash and sweep it
Blue again.

— *Dorothy Aldis*

Rain of Leaves

It's raining big,
it's raining small,
it's raining autumn leaves
in fall.

It's raining gold
and red and brown
as autumn leaves
come raining down.

It's raining everywhere
I look.
It's raining bookmarks
on my book!

— *Aileen Fisher*

Haiku

Little frog among
rain-shaken leaves, are you, too,
splashed with fresh, green paint?

— *Gaki*

Aogaeru onore mo penki nuritate ka

hose

The hose
Can squeeze
Water to
A silver rod
That digs
Hard holes
In the mud,

Or, muzzled
Tighter by
The nozzle,
Can rain
Chill diamond
Chains
Across the yard,

Or, fanned
Out fine,
Can hang
A silk
Rainbow
Halo
Over soft fog.

— *Valerie Worth*

Bubbles

Two bubbles found they had rainbows on their curves.
They flickered out saying:
"It was worth being a bubble just to have held that
rainbow thirty seconds."

— *Carl Sandburg*

The Secret Place

It was my secret place—
  down at the foot
  of my bed—
  under the covers.

It was very white.

I went there
  with a book, a flashlight,
  and the special pencil
  that my grandfather gave me.

To read—
  and to draw pictures
  on all that white.

It was my secret place
  for about a week—

Until my mother came
  to change the sheets.

                — *Tomie dePaola*

Secret Door

The upstairs room
has a secret door.
Dad says someone
used it for
some papers many years ago,
and if I want to, I can go
and bring a treasured thing
to hide and lock it up
all dark inside

and it can be
a place for me
to open
with
its
tiny
key.

— Myra Cohn Livingston

The Island

They mowed the meadow down below
Our house the other day
But left a grassy island where
We still can go and play.

Right in the middle of the field
It rises green and high;
Bees swing on the clover there,
And butterflies blow by.

It seems a very far-off place
With oceans all around:
The only thing to see is sky,
And wind, the only sound.

— *Dorothy Aldis*

Hideout

They looked for me
and from my nook
inside the oak
I watched them look.

Through little slits
between the leaves
I saw their looking
legs and sleeves.

They would have looked
all over town
except—
I threw some acorns down.

— *Aileen Fisher*

We're Racing, Racing down the Walk

We're racing, racing down the walk,
Over the pavement and round the block.
We rumble along till the sidewalk ends—
Felicia and I and half our friends.
Our hair flies backward. It's whish and whirr!
She roars at me and I shout at her
As past the porches and garden gates
We rattle and rock
On our roller skates.

— *Phyllis McGinley*

All Wet

Tommy had a water gun.
He squirted it at Jimmy,
at Jamey, George, and Jennifer,
and Katie, Kim and Timmy.
He squirted Sally on the nose.
He squirted Molly on the toes.
He laughed and thought it
lots of fun
till—
Sammy got him
with the hose.

— *Tony Johnston*

Overdog

Overdog Johnson is a guy
who always wins
but hardly tries.

Pitcher sails it.
Johnson nails it.
Whack!
Homerun!

Pitcher steams it.
Johnson creams it.
Thwack!
Homerun!

Pitcher smokes it.
Johnson pokes it.
Smack!
Homerun!

Pitcher fires it.
Johnson wires it.
Crack!
Ho-hum.

— *Tony Johnston*

Queenie

Queenie's strong and Queenie's tall.
You should see her bat a ball,
Ride a bike, or climb a wall.
(Queenie's not her name at all.)

Queenie's nimble, Queenie's quick.
You should see her throw a stick,
Watch her saw a board that's thick,
See her do her tumbling trick.

Queenie's not afraid, like me,
Of snakes or climbing up a tree.
(I think that's why the boys agree,
Queenie's what her name should be.)

— *Leland B. Jacobs*

29

The Witch

She comes by night, in fearsome flight,
in garments black as pitch,
the queen of doom upon her broom,
the wild and wicked witch,

a cackling crone with brittle bones
and desiccated limbs,
two evil eyes with warts and sties
and bags about the rims,

a dangling nose, ten twisted toes
and folds of shrivelled skin,
cracked and chipped and crackled lips
that frame a toothless grin.

She hurtles by, she sweeps the sky
and hurls a piercing screech.
As she swoops past, a spell is cast
on all her curses reach.

Take care to hide when the wild witch rides
to shriek her evil spell.
What she may do with a word or two
is much too grim to tell.

— *Jack Prelutsky*

Ghoulies and Ghosties

From ghoulies and ghosties,
Long-leggity beasties,
And things that go *bump* in the night,
Good Lord deliver us.

— Old spell

My Brother

My brother is inside the sheet
That gave that awful shout.
I know because those are his feet
So brown and sticking out.

And that's his head that waggles there
And his eyes peeking through—
So I can laugh, so I don't care:
"Ha!" I say. "It's you."

— Dorothy Aldis

A Good Play

We built a ship upon the stairs
All made of the back-bedroom chairs,
And filled it full of sofa pillows
To go a-sailing on the billows.

We took a saw and several nails,
And water in the nursery pails;
And Tom said, "Let us also take
An apple and a slice of cake";
Which was enough for Tom and me
To go a-sailing on, till tea.

We sailed along for days and days
And had the very best of plays;
But Tom fell out and hurt his knee,
So there was no one left but me.

— *Robert Louis Stevenson*

back yard

Sun in the back yard
Grows lazy,

Dozing on the porch steps
All morning,

Getting up and nosing
About corners,

Gazing into an empty
Flowerpot,

Later easing over the grass
For a nap,

Unless
Someone hangs out the wash—

Which changes
Everything to a rush and clap

Of wet
Cloth, and fresh wind

And sun
Wide awake in the white sheets.

— *Valerie Worth*

Worlds I Know

I can read the pictures
by myself
in the books that lie
on the lowest shelf.
I know the place
where the stories start
and some I can even say
by heart,
and I make up adventures
and dreams and words
for some of the pages
I've never heard.

But I like it best
when Mother sits
and reads to me
my favourites;
when Rapunzel pines
and the prince comes forth,
or the Snow Queen sighs
in the bitter north;
when Rose Red snuggles
against the bear,
and I lean against Mother
and feel her hair.

We look at stars
in Hungary—
back of the North Wind—
over the sea—
the Nutcracker laughs;
the Erl King calls;
a wish comes true;
the beanstalk falls;
the Western wind
blows sweet and low,
and Mother gives words
to worlds I know.

— *Myra Cohn Livingston*

The Walrus and the Carpenter

The sun was shining on the sea,
    Shining with all his might:
He did his very best to make
    The billows smooth and bright—
And this was odd, because it was
    The middle of the night.

The moon was shining sulkily,
    Because she thought the sun
Had got no business to be there
    After the day was done—
"It's very rude of him," she said,
    "To come and spoil the fun!"

The sea was wet as wet could be,
    The sands were dry as dry.
You could not see a cloud, because
    No cloud was in the sky;
No birds were flying overhead—
    There were no birds to fly.

WITH THANKS TO SIR JOHN TENNIEL

The Walrus and the Carpenter
　　Were walking close at hand:
They wept like anything to see
　　Such quantities of sand:
"If this were only cleared away,"
　　They said, "it would be grand!"

"If seven maids with seven mops
　　Swept it for half a year,
Do you suppose," the Walrus said,
　　"That they could get it clear?"
"I doubt it," said the Carpenter,
　　And shed a bitter tear.

"O Oysters, come and walk with us!"
　　The Walrus did beseech.
"A pleasant walk, a pleasant talk,
　　Along the briny beach:
We cannot do with more than four,
　　To give a hand to each."

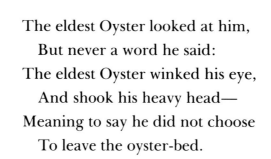

The eldest Oyster looked at him,
　　But never a word he said:
The eldest Oyster winked his eye,
　　And shook his heavy head—
Meaning to say he did not choose
　　To leave the oyster-bed.

But four young Oysters hurried up,
　　All eager for the treat:
Their coats were brushed, their faces washed,
　　Their shoes were clean and neat—
And this was odd, because, you know,
　　They hadn't any feet.

Four other Oysters followed them,
　　And yet another four;
And thick and fast they came at last,
　　And more, and more, and more—
All hopping through the frothy waves,
　　And scrambling to the shore.

The Walrus and the Carpenter
　　Walked on a mile or so,
And then they rested on a rock
　　Conveniently low:
And all the little Oysters stood
　　And waited in a row.

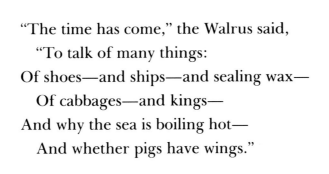

"The time has come," the Walrus said,
  "To talk of many things:
Of shoes—and ships—and sealing wax—
  Of cabbages—and kings—
And why the sea is boiling hot—
  And whether pigs have wings."

"But wait a bit," the Oysters cried,
  "Before we have our chat;
For some of us are out of breath,
  And all of us are fat!"
"No hurry!" said the Carpenter.
  They thanked him much for that.

"A loaf of bread," the Walrus said,
    "Is what we chiefly need:
Pepper and vinegar besides
    Are very good indeed—
Now, if you're ready, Oysters dear,
    We can begin to feed."

"But not on us!" the Oysters cried,
    Turning a little blue.
"After such kindness, that would be
    A dismal thing to do!"
"The night is fine," the Walrus said,
    "Do you admire the view?"

"It was so kind of you to come!
    And you are very nice!"
The Carpenter said nothing but
    "Cut us another slice.
I wish you were not quite so deaf—
    I've had to ask you twice!"

"It seems a shame," the Walrus said,
 "To play them such a trick.
After we've brought them out so far,
 And made them trot so quick!"
The Carpenter said nothing but
 "The butter's spread too thick!"

"I weep for you," the Walrus said:
 "I deeply sympathize."
With sobs and tears he sorted out
 Those of the largest size,
Holding his pocket-handkerchief
 Before his streaming eyes.

"O Oysters," said the Carpenter,
 "You've had a pleasant run!
Shall we be trotting home again?"
 But answer came there none—
And this was scarcely odd, because
 They'd eaten every one.
                              — *Lewis Carroll*

A House of Cards

A house of cards
    Is neat and small:
Shake the table,
    It must fall.
Find the Court cards
    One by one;
Raise it, roof it,—
    Now it's done:—
Shake the table!
    That's the fun.

      — *Christina Rossetti*

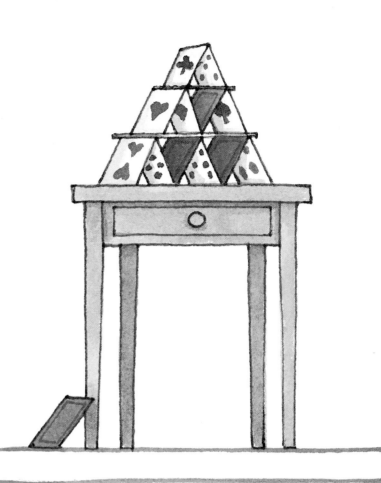

from Teddy Bear

A bear, however hard he tries,
Grows tubby without exercise.
Our Teddy Bear is short and fat
Which is not to be wondered at;
He gets what exercise he can
By falling off the ottoman,
But generally seems to lack
The energy to clamber back.

      — *A. A. Milne*

Silly Song

Mama.
I wish I were silver.

Son, you'd be very cold.

Mama.
I wish I were water.

Son, you'd be very cold.

Mama. Embroider me on your pillow.

That, yes!
Right away!

— *Federico Garcia Lorca*

Cancion Tonta

Mamá.
Yo quiero ser de plata.

Hijo,
tendrás mucho frio.

Mamá.
Yo quiero ser de agua.

Hijo,
tendrás mucho frio.

Mamá.
Bórdame en tu almohada.

¡Eso si!
¡Ahora mismo!

— *Federico Garcia Lorca*

Hallowe'en Indignation Meeting

A sulky witch and a surly cat
And a scowly owl and a skeleton sat
With a grouchy ghost and a waspish bat,
And angrily snarled and chewed the fat.

It seems they were all upset and riled
That they couldn't frighten the Modern Child,
Who was much too knowing and much too wild
And considered Hallowe'en spooks too mild.

Said the witch, "They call this the *human* race,
Yet the kiddies inhabit Outer Space;
They bob for comets, and eat ice cream
From flying saucers, to get up steam!"

"I'm a shade of my former self," said the skeleton.
"I shiver and shake like so much gelatin,
Indeed I'm a pitiful sight to see—
I'm scareder of *kids* than they are of *me*!"

— *Margaret Fishback*

44

The Moon's the North Wind's Cooky

What the Little Girl Said

The Moon's the North Wind's cooky.
He bites it, day by day,
Until there's but a rim of scraps
That crumble all away.

The South Wind is a baker.
He kneads clouds in his den,
And bakes a crisp new moon *that . . . greedy
North . . . Wind . . . eats . . . again!*

— *Vachel Lindsay*

Old Man Moon

The moon is very, very old.
The reason why is clear—
he gets a birthday once a month,
instead of once a year.

— *Aileen Fisher*

from The Wind and the Moon

Said the Wind to the Moon, "I will blow you out;
    You stare
    In the air
    Like a ghost in a chair,
Always looking what I am about—
I hate to be watched; I'll blow you out."

— *George MacDonald*

Bananas and Cream

Bananas and cream,
Bananas and cream:
All we could say was
Bananas and cream.

We couldn't say fruit,
We wouldn't say cow,
We didn't say sugar—
We don't say it now.

Bananas and cream,
Bananas and cream,
All we could shout was
Bananas and cream.

We didn't say why,
We didn't say how;
We forgot it was fruit,
We forgot the old cow;
We *never* said sugar,
We only said *WOW!*

Bananas and cream,
Bananas and cream;
All that we want is
Bananas and cream!

We didn't say dish,
We didn't say spoon;
We said not tomorrow,
But *NOW* and *HOW SOON!*

Bananas and cream,
Bananas and cream?
We yelled for bananas,
Bananas and scream!

— *David McCord*

48

The Little Girl and the Turkey

The little girl said
As she asked for more:
"But what is the Turkey
Thankful for?"

— *Dorothy Aldis*

Places to Hide a Secret Message

in a raindrop on a windowpane
in a moon shell
in a raisin in rice pudding

— *Eve Merriam*

The Land of Counterpane

When I was sick and lay abed,
I had two pillows at my head,
And all my toys beside me lay
To keep me happy all the day.

And sometimes for an hour or so,
I watched my leaden soldiers go,
With different uniforms and drills,
Among the bedclothes, through the hills;

And sometimes sent my ships in fleets
All up and down among the sheets;
Or brought my trees and houses out,
And planted cities all about.

I was the giant great and still
That sits upon the pillow-hill,
And sees before him, dale and plain,
The pleasant land of counterpane.

— *Robert Louis Stevenson*

Brother

I had a little brother
And I brought him to my mother
And I said I want another
Little brother for a change.

But she said don't be a bother
So I took him to my father
And I said this little bother
Of a brother's very strange.

But he said one little brother
Is exactly like another
And every little brother
Misbehaves a bit he said.

So I took the little bother
From my mother and my father
And I put the little bother
Of a brother back to bed.

— *Mary Ann Hoberman*

Little

I am the sister of him
And he is my brother.
He is too little for us
To talk to each other.

So every morning I show him
My doll and my book;
But every morning he still is
Too little to look.

— *Dorothy Aldis*

Some Things Don't
Make Any Sense at All

My mum says I'm her sugarplum.
My mum says I'm her lamb.
My mum says I'm completely perfect
Just the way I am.
My mum says I'm a super-special wonderful terrific little guy.
My mum just had another baby.
Why?

— *Judith Viorst*

basketball

when spanky goes
to the playground all the big boys say
   hey big time—what's happenin'
'cause his big brother plays basketball for their high school
and he gives them the power sign and says
   you got it
but when i go and say
   what's the word
they just say
   your nose is running junior

one day i'll be seven feet tall
even if i never get a big brother
and i'll stuff that sweaty ball down
their laughing throats

— *Nikki Giovanni*

Mother to Son

Well, son, I'll tell you:
Life for me ain't been no crystal stair.
It's had tacks in it,
And splinters,
And boards torn up,
And places with no carpet on the floor—
Bare.
But all the time
I'se been a-climbin' on,
And reachin' landin's,
And turnin' corners,
And sometimes goin' in the dark
Where there ain't been no light.
So, boy, don't you turn back.
Don't you set down on the steps
'Cause you find its kinder hard.
Don't you fall now—
For I'se still goin', honey,
I'se still climbin',
And life for me ain't been no crystal stair.

— Langston Hughes

To a Forgetful Wishing Well

All summer long, your round stone eardrum held
Wishes I whispered down you. None came true.
Didn't they make one ripple in your mind?
I even wished a silver pail for you.

— *X.J. Kennedy*

Poem

I loved my friend.
He went away from me.
There's nothing more to say.
The poem ends,
Soft as it began—
I loved my friend:

— *Langston Hughes*

A Small Discovery

Father,
Where do giants go to cry?

To the hills
Behind the thunder?
Or to the waterfall?
I wonder.

(Giants cry.
I know they do.
Do they wait
Till nighttime too?)

— *James A. Emanuel*

The Sugar Lady

There is an old lady who lives down the hall,
Wrinkled and grey and toothless and small.
At seven already she's up,
Going from door to door with a cup.
"Do you have any sugar?" she asks,
Although she's got more than you.
"Do you have any sugar," she asks,
Hoping you'll talk for a minute or two.

— *Frank Asch*

Growing Old

When I grow old I hope to be
As beautiful as Grandma Lee.
Her hair is soft and fluffy white.
Her eyes are blue and candle bright.
And down her cheeks are cunning piles
Of little ripples when she smiles.

— *Rose Henderson*

Dunce Song 6

Her hand in my hand,
Soft as the south wind,
Soft as a colt's nose,
Soft as forgetting;

Her cheek to my cheek,
Red as the cranberry,
Red as a mitten,
Red as remembering—

Here we go round like raindrops,
Raindrops,
Here we go round
So snug together,

Oh, but I wonder,
Oh, but I know,
Who comforts like raisins,
Who kisses like snow.

— *Mark Van Doren*

Old Noah's Ark

Old Noah once he built an ark,
And patched it up with hickory bark.
He anchored it to a great big rock,
And then he began to load his stock.
The animals went in one by one,
The elephant chewing a carroway bun.
The animals went in two by two,
The crocodile and the kangaroo.
The animals went in three by three,
The tall giraffe and the tiny flea,
The animals went in four by four,
The hippopotamus stuck in the door.
The animals went in five by five,
The bees mistook the bear for a hive.
The animals went in six by six,
The monkey was up to his usual tricks.
The animals went in seven by seven,
Said the ant to the elephant, "Who're ye shov'n?"
The animals went in eight by eight,
Some were early and some were late.
The animals went in nine by nine,
They all formed fours and marched in a line.
The animals went in ten by ten,
If you want any more, you can read it again.

— Folk rhyme

The Song of the Mischievous Dog

There are many who say that a dog has its day,
    And a cat has a number of lives;
There are others who think that a lobster is pink,
    And that bees never work in their hives.
There are fewer, of course, who insist that a horse
    Has a horn and two humps on its head,
And a fellow who jests that a mare can build nests
    Is as rare as a donkey that's red.
Yet in spite of all this, I have moments of bliss,
    For I cherish a passion for bones,
And though doubtful of biscuit, I'm willing to risk it,
    And love to chase rabbits and stones.
But my greatest delight is to take a good bite
    At a calf that is plump and delicious;
And if I indulge in a bite at a bulge,
    Let's hope you won't think me too vicious.

— *Dylan Thomas, age 11*

The Panther

The panther is like a leopard,
Except it hasn't been peppered.
Should you behold a panther crouch,
Prepare to say Ouch.
Better yet, if called by a panther,
Don't anther.

— *Ogden Nash*

I Speak, I Say, I Talk

Cats purr.
Lions roar.
Owls hoot.
Bears snore.
Crickets creak.
Mice squeak.
Sheep baa.
But I SPEAK!

Monkeys chatter.
Cows moo.
Ducks quack.
Doves coo.
Pigs squeal.
Horses neigh.
Chickens cluck.
But I SAY!

Flies hum.
Dogs growl.
Bats screech.
Coyotes howl.
Frogs croak.
Parrots squawk.
Bees buzz.
But I TALK!

— *Arnold L. Shapiro*

Eagle Flight

An eagle wings gracefully
    through the sky.
On the earth I stand
    and watch.
My heart flies with it.

— *Alonzo Lopez*

The Blackbird

In the far corner
close by the swings,
every morning
a blackbird sings.

His bill's so yellow,
his coat's so black,
that he makes a fellow
whistle back.

Ann, my daughter,
thinks that he
sings for us two
especially.

— *Humbert Wolfe*

The Song of the Jellicles

Jellicle Cats come out to-night,
Jellicle Cats come one come all:
The Jellicle Moon is shining bright—
Jellicles come to the Jellicle Ball.

Jellicle Cats are black and white,
Jellicle Cats are rather small;
Jellicle Cats are merry and bright,
And pleasant to hear when they caterwaul.
Jellicle Cats have cheerful faces,
Jellicle Cats have bright black eyes;
They like to practise their airs and graces
And wait for the Jellicle Moon to rise.

Jellicle Cats develop slowly,
Jellicle Cats are not too big;
Jellicle Cats are roly-poly,
They know how to dance a gavotte and a jig.
Until the Jellicle Moon appears
They make their toilette and take their repose:
Jellicles wash behind their ears,
Jellicles dry between their toes.

Jellicle Cats are white and black,
Jellicle Cats are of moderate size;
Jellicles jump like a jumping-jack,
Jellicle Cats have moonlit eyes.
They're quiet enough in the morning hours,
They're quiet enough in the afternoon,
Reserving their terpsichorean powers
To dance by the light of the Jellicle Moon.

Jellicle Cats are black and white,
Jellicle Cats (as I said) are small;
If it happens to be a stormy night
They will practise a caper or two in the hall.
If it happens the sun is shining bright
You would say they had nothing to do at all:
They are resting and saving themselves to be right
For the Jellicle Moon and the Jellicle Ball.

— *T. S. Eliot*

Alligator on the Escalator

Through the revolving door
Of a department store
There slithered an alligator.

When he came to the escalator,
He stepped upon the track with great dexterity;
His tail draped over the railing,
And he clicked his teeth in glee:
  "Yo, I'm off on the escalator,
  Excited as I can be!
  It's a *moving* experience,
  As you can plainly see.

On the moving stair I go anywhere,
I rise to the top
Past outerwear, innerwear,
Dinnerwear, thinnerwear—
Then down to the basement with bargains galore,
Then back on the track to the top once more!
Oh, I may ride the escalator
Until closing time or later,
So tell the telephone operator
To call Mrs. Albert Q. Alligator
And tell her to take a hot mud bath
And not to wait up for me!"

— *Eve Merriam*

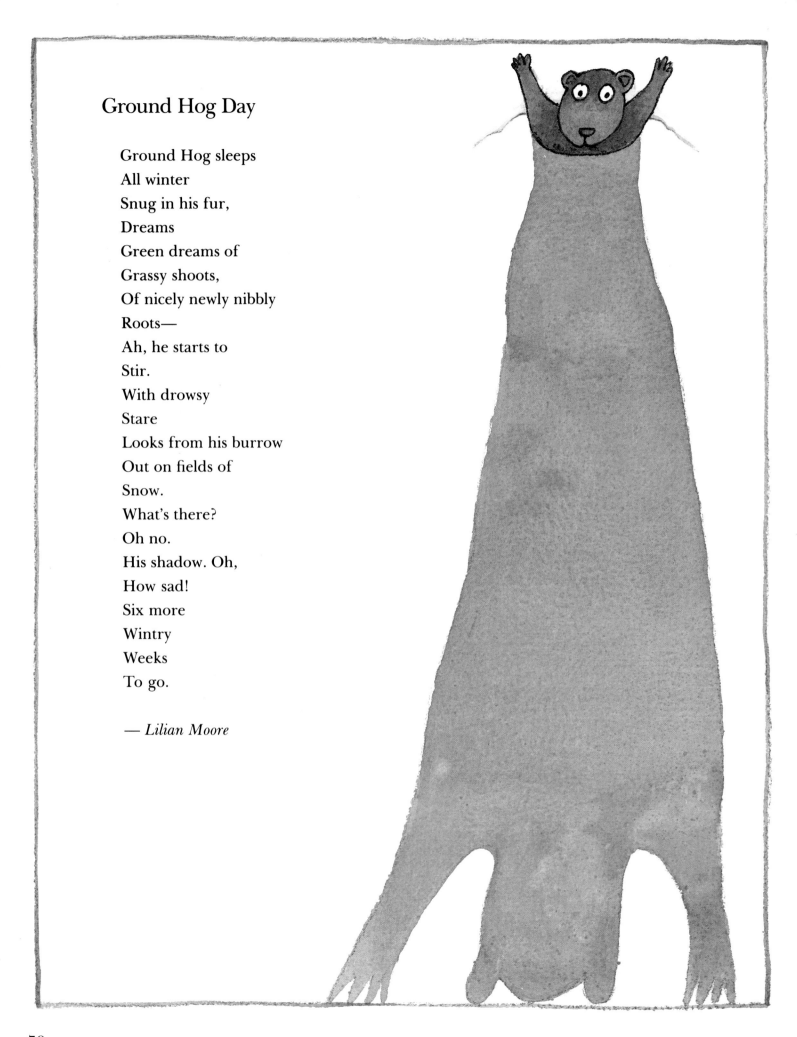

Ground Hog Day

Ground Hog sleeps
All winter
Snug in his fur,
Dreams
Green dreams of
Grassy shoots,
Of nicely newly nibbly
Roots—
Ah, he starts to
Stir.
With drowsy
Stare
Looks from his burrow
Out on fields of
Snow.
What's there?
Oh no.
His shadow. Oh,
How sad!
Six more
Wintry
Weeks
To go.

— *Lilian Moore*

Singing

Little birds sing with their beaks
In the apple trees;
But little crickets in the grass
Are singing with their knees.

— *Dorothy Aldis*

Dandelion

O little soldier with the golden helmet,
What are you guarding on my lawn?
You with your green gun
And your yellow beard,
Why do you stand so stiff?
There is only the grass to fight!

— *Hilda Conkling*

The Three Foxes

Once upon a time there were three little foxes
Who didn't wear stockings, and they didn't wear sockses,
But they all had handkerchiefs to blow their noses,
And they kept their handkerchiefs in cardboard boxes.

They lived in the forest in three little houses,
And they didn't wear coats, and they didn't wear trousies.
They ran through the woods on their little bare tootsies,
And they played "Touch last" with a family of mouses.

They didn't go shopping in the High Street shopses,
But caught what they wanted in the woods and copses.
They all went fishing, and they caught three wormses,
They went out hunting, and they caught three wopses.

They went to a Fair, and they all won prizes—
Three plum-puddings and three mince-pieses.
They rode on elephants and swang on swingses,
And hit three coco-nuts at coco-nut shieses.

That's all that I know of the three little foxes
Who kept their handkerchiefs in cardboard boxes.
They lived in the forest in three little houses,
But they didn't wear coats and they didn't wear trousies,
And they didn't wear stockings and they didn't wear sockses.

— *A. A. Milne*

Busy Summer

Bees
make wax and honey,

Spiders,
webs of silk.

Wasps
make paper houses.

Cows
make cream and milk.

Dandelions
make pollen
for the bees to take.

Wish that I
had something
I knew how to make.

— *Aileen Fisher*

Open Hydrant

Water rushes up
and gushes,
cooling summer's sizzle.

In a sudden whoosh
it rushes,
not a little drizzle.

First a hush and down
it crashes,
over curbs it swishes.

Just a luscious waterfall
for
cooling city fishes.

— *Marci Ridlon*

The Balloon Man

Our balloon man has balloons.
He holds them on a string.
He blows his horn and walks about
Through puddles, in the spring.

He stands on corners while they bob
And tug above his head—
Green balloons and blue balloons
And yellow ones, and red.

He takes our pennies and unties
The two we choose; and then
He turns around, and waves his hand,
And blows his horn again.

— *Dorothy Aldis*

76

The Hungry Waves

The hungry waves along the shore
Chase each other with a roar.

They raise their heads and, wide and high,
Toss their hair against the sky.

They show their teeth in rows of white
And open up their jaws to bite.

— *Dorothy Aldis*

The Caterpillar

Brown and furry
Caterpillar in a hurry,
Take your walk
To the shady leaf, or stalk,
    Or what not,
Which may be the chosen spot.
    No toad spy you,
Hovering bird of prey pass by you;
Spin and die,
To live again a butterfly.

— *Christina Rossetti*

Haiku

A discovery!
On my frog's smooth, green belly
there sits no button.

— *Yayû*

Mitsuketari, kawazu ni heso no naki koto o

Snail

They have brought me a snail.

Inside it sings
a map-green ocean.
My heart
swells with water,
with small fish
of brown and silver.

They have brought me a snail.

— *Federico Garcia Lorca*

Caracola

Me han traido una caracola.

Dentro le canta
un mar de mapa.
Mi corazón
se llena de agua,
con pececillos
de sombra y plata.

Me han traido una caracola.

— *Federico Garcia Lorca*

Cat in Moonlight

Through moonlight's milk
She slowly passes
As soft as silk
Between tall grasses.
I watch her go
So sleek and white,
As white as snow,
The moon so bright
I hardly know
White moon, white fur,
Which is the light
And which is her.

— *Douglas Gibson*

Fog

The fog comes
on little cat feet.

It sits looking
over harbour and city
on silent haunches
and then moves on.

— *Carl Sandburg*

Flowers at Night

Some flowers close their petals,
blue and red and bright,
and go to sleep all tucked away
inside themselves at night.

Some flowers leave their petals
like windows open wide
so they can watch the goings-on
of stars and things outside.

— *Aileen Fisher*

The Swallow

Fly away, fly away, over the sea,
Sun-loving swallow, for summer is done.
Come again, come again, come back to me,
Bringing the summer and bringing the sun.

— *Christina Rossetti*

Autumn Leaves

One of the nicest beds I know
isn't a bed of soft white snow,
isn't a bed of cool green grass
after the noisy mowers pass,
isn't a bed of yellow hay
making me itch for half a day—
but autumn leaves in a pile *that* high,
deep, and smelling like fall, and dry.
That's the bed where I like to lie
and watch the flutters go by.

— *Aileen Fisher*

Dragon Smoke

Breathe and blow
white clouds
    with every puff.
It's cold today,
    cold enough
to see your breath.
Huff!
    Breathe dragon smoke
      today!

          — *Lilian Moore*

Autumn

The morns are meeker than they were,
The berry's cheek is plumper,
The nuts are getting brown;
The rose is out of town.

The maple wears a gayer scarf,
The field a scarlet gown.
Lest I should be old-fashioned
I'll put a trinket on.

          — *Emily Dickinson*

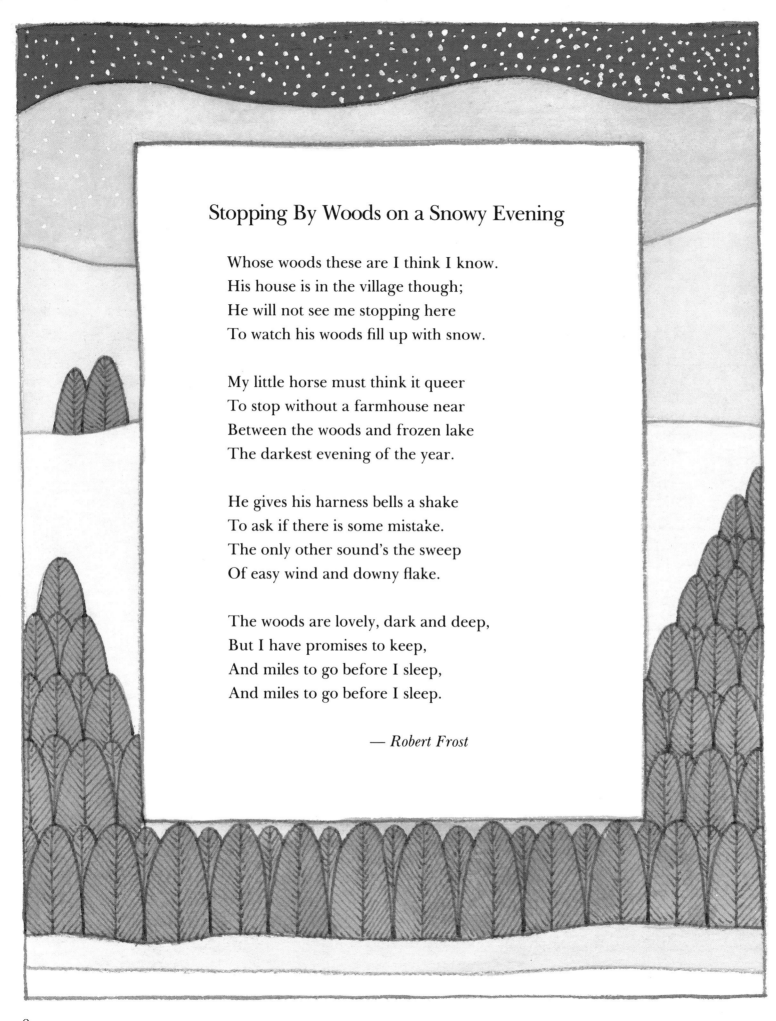

Stopping By Woods on a Snowy Evening

Whose woods these are I think I know.
His house is in the village though;
He will not see me stopping here
To watch his woods fill up with snow.

My little horse must think it queer
To stop without a farmhouse near
Between the woods and frozen lake
The darkest evening of the year.

He gives his harness bells a shake
To ask if there is some mistake.
The only other sound's the sweep
Of easy wind and downy flake.

The woods are lovely, dark and deep,
But I have promises to keep,
And miles to go before I sleep,
And miles to go before I sleep.

— Robert Frost

City Lights

Into the endless dark
The lights of the buildings shine,
Row upon twinkling row,
Line upon glistening line.
Up and up they mount
Till the tallest seems to be
The topmost taper set
On a towering Christmas tree.

— *Rachel Field*

Window

Night from a railroad car window
Is a great, dark, soft thing
Broken across with slashes of light.

— *Carl Sandburg*

Dream Variation

To fling my arms wide
In some place of the sun,
To whirl and to dance
Till the white day is done.
Then rest at cool evening
Beneath a tall tree
While night comes on gently,
   Dark like me—
That is my dream!

To fling my arms wide
In the face of the sun,
Dance! Whirl! Whirl!
Till the quick day is done.
Rest at pale evening . . .
A tall, slim tree . . .
Night coming tenderly
   Black like me.

— *Langston Hughes*

Bed in Summer

In winter I get up at night
And dress by yellow candlelight.
In summer, quite the other way,
I have to go to bed by day.

I have to go to bed and see
The birds still hopping on the tree,
Or hear the grown-up people's feet
Still going past me in the street.

And does it not seem hard to you,
When all the sky is clear and blue,
And I should like so much to play,
To have to go to bed by day?

— *Robert Louis Stevenson*

Covers

Glass covers windows
   to keep the cold away
Clouds cover the sky
   to make a rainy day

Nighttime covers
   all the things that creep
Blankets cover me
   when I'm asleep

— *Nikki Giovanni*

Little Donkey Close Your Eyes

Little Donkey on the hill
Standing there so very still
Making faces at the skies
Little Donkey close your eyes.

Little Monkey in the tree
Swinging there so merrily
Throwing coconuts at the skies
Little Monkey close your eyes.

Silly Sheep that slowly crop
Night has come and you must stop
Chewing grass beneath the skies
Little Sheep now close your eyes.

Little Pig that squeals about
Make no noises with your snout
No more squealing to the skies
Little Pig now close your eyes.

Wild young birds that sweetly sing
Curve your heads beneath your wing
Dark night covers all the skies
Wild young birds now close your eyes.

Old black cat down in the barn
Keeping five small kittens warm
Let the wind blow in the skies
Dear old black cat close your eyes.

Little child all tucked in bed
Looking such a sleepy head
Stars are quiet in the skies
Little child now close your eyes.

— *Margaret Wise Brown*

Copyright Acknowledgments

Index of First Lines

A bear, however hard he tries, 42
A birdie with a yellow bill, 13
A discovery!, 78
A house of cards, 42
A sulky witch and a surly cat, 44
All summer long, your round stone eardrum held, 56
An eagle wings gracefully, 65

Bananas and cream, 48
Bees make wax and honey, 74
Breathe and blow, 83
Brown and furry, 78

Cats purr., 64

Don't you ever, 14

Father, Where do giants go to cry?, 57
Fly away, fly away, over the sea, 82
From ghoulies and ghosties, 31

Glass covers windows, 89
Ground Hog sleeps, 70

Her hand in my hand, 59

I am the sister of him, 53
I can read the pictures, 34
I had a little brother, 52
I loved my friend., 56
I shall dance tonight., 15
in a raindrop on a windowpane, 49
In my bed all safe and warm, 16
In the far corner, 65

In winter I get up at night, 88
Into the endless dark, 86
It's raining big, 19
It was my secret place—, 22

Jellicle Cats come out to-night—, 66

Little birds sing with their beaks, 71
Little Donkey on the hill, 90
Little frog among, 19

Mama., 43
Mamá., 43
Me han traido una caracola., 79
My brother is inside the sheet, 31
My mum says I'm her sugarplum., 53

Night from a railroad car window, 86

O little soldier with the golden helmet, 71
Old Noah once he built an ark, 61
On stormy days, 18
Once upon a time there were three little foxes, 73
One of the nicest beds I know, 82
Our balloon man has balloons., 76
Overdog Johnson is a guy, 28

Piping down the valleys wild, 11

Queenie's strong and Queenie's tall., 29

Said the Wind to the Moon, "I will blow you out;, 47
Sandpaper kisses, 13
She comes by night, in fearsome flight, 30

Some flowers close their petals, 81
Sun in the back yard, 33

The fog comes, 81
The hose, 20
The hungry waves along the shore, 77
The little girl said, 49
The moon is very, very old., 47
The Moon's the North Wind's cooky., 46
The morns are meeker than they were, 83
The panther is like a leopard, 63
The sun was shining on the sea, 36
The upstairs room, 23
The way to start a day is this—, 12
There are many who say that a dog has its day, 62
There is an old lady who lives down the hall, 58
There is no frigate like a book, 9
They have brought me a snail., 79

They looked for me, 25
They mowed the meadow down below, 24
Through moonlight's milk, 80
Through the revolving door, 68
To fling my arms wide, 87
Tommy had a water gun., 27
Two bubbles found they had
    rainbows on their curves., 21

Water rushes up, 75
We built a ship upon the stairs, 32
Well, son, I'll tell you:, 55
We're racing, racing down the walk, 26
When I grow old I hope to be, 58
When I was sick and lay abed, 51
when Spanky goes, 54
Whenever the moon and stars are set, 17
Whose woods these are I think I know., 84